Stand

The Stories and Scriptures

What Readers Are Saying

The best songs are not the ones that just sound good but are lived well. Sharon takes her stories and what God is teaching her and puts it to music and it is awesome. "Stand" tells the stories of God working in her life and how each song was written because of a story. We all struggle with the same issues and challenges in life though our specific circumstances may be different. I wholeheartedly endorse and encourage you to not just hear her music but to know her stories as well. When you do that, the music will be even more powerful.

Bob Roberts, Jr.
Pastor, Author, Glocal Engager
northwoodchurch.org; glocal.net

Have you ever heard a beautiful song, with words that lodged in your heart and wondered, "I'd love to know the story that birthed that!" Singer/songwriter Sharon Tedford has lifted the veil and welcomed us into the process, revealing the stories behind the songs of her. The lyrics flow not from a desire simply to tell the reader about her Jesus. Instead, she discloses the intimate relationship she enjoys with the Savior, and invites us to join her there. Well-written and compelling, Tedford weaves stories that tempt the reader to set the book aside and sit for a while at the feet of the King. The companion CD is the perfect accompaniment for that time with Him. Do not miss this powerful and inspiring book.

Deborah DeArmond
Author <i>Don't Go to Bed Angry, Stay Up and Fight</i>
DebDeArmond.com

For many years I worked with Sharon Tedford she as the worship leader and me as the senior pastor of the church. Her thoughtful, careful and spiritual leadership of corporate acts of worship were a constant inspiration. These songs, and the stories that accompany them, resonate with the same deep spirituality. The words and the music will inspire prayer and praise, leading to wholeness and increasing discipleship. Sharon's songs are biblically based and practically potent. I commend them to you for both private and public worship. This book will feed your soul and the biblical truths will strengthen your walk with God.

Stephen Gaukroger
Pastor, Author, Director – Clarion Trust International
clariontrust.org.uk

Thanks

Jon John Robinson, your constant refrain of, "People need to hear the stories behind these songs!" is what breathed life into this book. Thank you for your constant encouragement and frequent reminders that God always has more for us. This book is definitely a reflection of that "more".

Jennifer Hunt, your kind expertise and frugal way with words was just what I needed, as you edited my book with me and pulled out the finer things of the "English" language. You know that we will forever disagree on spelling and pronunciation, but this book has finesse largely because of you. Thank you.

To the few who read over the early drafts (Kelly, Dana, Jan, and Gareth), thank you for helping me to refine the stories. I am grateful for your thoughts and support.

Kathy, I'm so thankful for your eye for detail and your willingness to lend your design expertise to this project. Thank you!

Profound thanks to the Corey family, for allowing me to share the extraordinary story of their son and brother. Nathan has changed my life forever, and I pray that his story will change others too.

Jon and Jordan Busk, thank you for allowing me to be a small part of your wedding day. The song I wrote for you is also my prayer for you–may you always run after Jesus, both together and as individuals, as He perfects your faith.

Danny, Kirsty, Carolyn, Richard and Maria, your kindness in giving me the freedom to share your stories is sincerely appreciated. It is my desire that many will find release and truth in the fact that there is power in a prayer.

Joseph, Pippa and Roo, I am honored to call you my children. You hardly batted an eyelid when this project began and you behaved as if it were a completely normal thing to do. That attitude is inspiring and your backing and enjoyment of what you read humbles me.

Gareth, my favorite husband, you cheer me on like none other. You have reassured me and taken care of the "boring stuff" with excellence. If it weren't for you, this book would still be a file on my computer. God knew what He was doing when He put us together. You bless me.

To my parents, Terry and Viv - You have always been behind me and have supported my years of development as an artist and writer. I am indebted to you both. Thank you for loving each other well, and for loving Jesus unceasingly.

Ephesians 3:20-21 expresses my final thanks best:
"Now to him who is able to do **immeasurably more** than all we ask or imagine, according to his power that is at work within us, to him be glory in the church and in Christ Jesus throughout all generations, for ever and ever! Amen."

Stand

The Stories and Scriptures

The stories behind the
songs and the Scriptures
that gave them foundation.

By Sharon Tedford

A 61Things Publication

Stand. The Stories and Scriptures
Copyright © 2017 by Sharon Tedford

All rights reserved. No part of this publication may be reproduced, stored in a retrieval system, or transmitted in any form by any means – electronic, mechanical, photocopy, recording, or any other without the prior permission of the publisher.

Published by 61 Things LLC, Southlake, Texas, USA
www.61-Things.com   Reference: 61TDC-BK1

ISBN: 978-0-578-18911-6

All songs written by Sharon Tedford. 'This Is Our Prayer' Vamp co-written with Marquinn Middleton. Used by permission.
Lyrics & Sound Recording © ℗ 61 Things LLC, 2017.

All Scripture quotations, unless otherwise identified, are taken from The Holy Bible, *New International Version®, NIV®*, Copyright © 1973, 1978, 1984, 2011 by Biblica, Inc.™ Used by Permission. All rights reserved worldwide.

Scripture quotations marked ESV are taken from *The Holy Bible, English Standard Version®, ESV®* Bible, Copyright © 2001 by Crossway, a publishing ministry of Good News Publishers. Used by Permission. All rights reserved.

Scripture quotations marked NASB are taken from the *New American Standard Bible®*, Copyright © 1960, 1962, 1963, 1968, 1971, 1972, 1972, 1975, 1977, 1995 by The Lockman Foundation. Used by permission.

Scripture quotations marked NLT are taken from the *Holy Bible, New Living Translation,* Copyright © 1996, 2004, 2007 by Tyndale House Foundation. Used by permission of Tyndale House Publishers, Inc..

Scripture quotations marked KJV are taken from *The Holy Bible, King James Version.* Cambridge Edition: 1769; King James Bible Online, 2016.
www.kingjamesbibleonline.org.

Edited by: Jennifer Hunt
Cover Photo by: Felicia Johns @ HeartBoxWeddings.com
Cover Design by: Kathy Gunnels
Interior layout and design by: Gareth Tedford

Contents

Introduction	Stand. The Stories and Scriptures	11
One	Stand. Still.	15
Two	Perfect Rest (Nate's Song)	27
Three	Shepherd King	37
Four	This Is Our Prayer	49
Five	Devotion	59
Six	In The Secret of The Stable	67
Seven	Father of All Days	75
Eight	The Power of a Prayer	83
Nine	Perfecter of Our Faith	93
Ten	Oil of Blessing	103
Epilogue		113
References		119
Stand, the CD		121

Introduction

Stand. The Stories and Scriptures

I'm very keen that you know this about me: I'm just an ordinary girl from England. I'm a wife trying to be a better example of Jesus to my fabulous husband. I'm a mum trying to raise three kids. I love my husband and our children with all my heart, but sometimes (too often!) I let myself get in the way of what God wants to do in me and through me. I am not perfect, but I am perfectly loved by a Heavenly Father who desires relationship with all of His children.

God has unfolded these songs and their stories over a seven-year period. The stories I tell here are an extract of my life, mere snippets of different thought processes and seasons. I don't get new songs every day. The natural cadence to my relationship with the Father includes both good and bad days, flawed and evolving—which I imagine is much like yours.

I love Jesus. I want to love Him more. My life is intentionally pointed in the direction of Jesus, because He is my goal.

This project has led me to a new place of understanding the word "stand." There is so much in the Bible about standing. God has a tight hold of those who love Him, and we only have to *stand* on the unmovable foundation of that truth. When all around looks bleak, *stand* on the fact that God is in control. When you know the Father is calling you to be a representation for Him, *stand* and bravely express His love to those around you. When you are mentally, emotionally and physically exhausted, *stand* still and allow God to work. To stand is an action. It is not passive. Even if all we do for a while is *stand,* we are still actively engaging in this battle of life.

I sincerely hope as you read the stories you will recognize God's voice speaking life into your own story. I pray you will engage with Him in a new way and learn again what it is to **stand**.

Ephesians 6:13
Therefore put on the full armor of God, so that when the day of evil comes, you may be able to **stand** your ground, and after you have done everything, to stand.

1 Corinthians 16:13
Be on your guard; **stand** firm in the faith; be courageous; be strong.

1 Corinthians 15:58
Therefore, my dear brothers and sisters, **stand** firm. Let nothing move you. Always give yourselves fully to the work of the Lord, because you know that your labor in the Lord is not in vain.

Galatians 5:1
It is for freedom that Christ has set us free. **Stand** firm, then, and do not let yourselves be burdened again by a yoke of slavery.

2 Chronicles 20:17
You will not have to fight this battle. Take up your positions; **stand** firm and see the deliverance the LORD will give you, Judah and Jerusalem. Do not be afraid; do not be discouraged. Go out to face them tomorrow, and the LORD will be with you.

Exodus 14:13 (NLT)
Don't be afraid. Just **stand** still and watch the LORD rescue you today.

Proverbs 10:25
When the storm has swept by, the wicked are gone, but the righteous **stand** firm forever.

One

Stand. Still.

The Song:

My heart waits for you Lord
My soul longs for you Lord
All my hope comes from you
So I'll wait, I'll wait for you Lord.

Chorus:
And I'll stand, still in your presence
Yes I'll see what you will do
I'll be still, patiently waiting
And worshiping you - Jesus
Yes, I'll stand, still in your presence
And I'll fix my eyes on you
I'll be still quietly resting
And trusting in you Jesus.

Bridge:
Come fill me again
With all of your fire
Come fill me again
It's you I desire
Come fill me again
And make me brand new
Come fill me again
Only with you.

I'll be still
I'll be quiet
I will trust
I will wait

The Story: Stand. Still

Perhaps no two words lie closer to my heart than these: Stand. Still.

Early in our marriage we, like many of you, had a miscarriage. In fact, we had two miscarriages before we had our first son. This third pregnancy was terribly difficult for me. I spent many of those early days terrified of what the day would bring. I experienced a confusing mix of joyful celebration and dragging anxiety. There was very little I could do to control the circumstance, and I look back on that period as the time when the Father really got my attention. During a Sunday service Gareth and I both felt the Lord speak to us through this Scripture:

> "You will not have to fight this battle. Take up your positions; **stand firm** and see the deliverance the Lord will give you, Judah and Jerusalem. Do not be afraid; do not be discouraged. Go out to face them tomorrow, and the Lord will be with you." (2 Chronicles 20:17, emphasis mine).

I was trying to fight this "battle" on my own, with my own understanding and choices. I was painfully aware of my empty armory of weapons, and I was terrified of once again facing defeat. But God revealed to us, loud and clear, we must hand over our fear to Him and allow Him to be the one who would "deliver" this baby. I had to learn not to be afraid. It wasn't a button I could simply push. Throughout the pregnancy I repeatedly had reason to fear. However, I would return to our little kitchen in our first apartment and read that Scripture, written on a small card and posted on our kitchen cabinet. (I still have that dog-eared piece of paper, and throughout the years, it has found itself stuck on the mirrors and cabinets of three houses!) I had to choose to surrender a fight that was never meant to be mine, put down my weapons of anger and uncertainty, and allow the Father to fight this battle for us. My job (and believe me, it often felt like work) was to *stand*.

My "stand" in this instance was not passive in any way. I made a very active choice. I was electing to allow God to have His place, to make a way for our son to be safe, to bring (literal) deliverance to our little family. I was exercising my right as a child of the King, to stand in His presence and watch Him work out His perfect plan. I wasn't backed into a corner, or subbed out to the bench. I wasn't a bystander or a lifeless observer. No, I was filled with life—both mine and that of our son. My decisive action was obedience. I obeyed God's command to "stand firm and see…" I was absolutely not ready to sit down, bow out, or disappear from the scene, nor did God ever ask me to. The Father wanted me to actively witness His great power and might. I still had to face the circumstance, but the Lord had promised to be with me. My job during that time was to trust, obey, and pray. And that's just what I did. Today our son is a healthy and remarkable eighteen year old.

Stand can also imply resistance. Believing in Jesus often requires us to battle evil. Ephesians 6:12-13 reminds us

> "...our struggle is not against flesh and blood, but against the rulers, against the authorities, against the powers of this dark world and against the spiritual forces of evil in the heavenly realms. Therefore put on the full armor of God, so that when the day of evil comes, you may be able to stand your ground, and after you have done everything, to stand."

The two words for "stand" translated here are actually two different Greek words. The first time we see "to stand" it is better translated as *withstand*, or *to stand your ground*. That can also be recognized as *resist* or *to set against*. The second "to stand" can be unraveled a bit more to mean *stand still, establish, to place, to make firm and abide*.

In modern vernacular, we might say, "He stood there and did not join in." That's clearly not what Paul, the writer of Ephesians, is implying. In fact, he is urging us to respond to the works of the enemy with *action*. We are called to stand our ground when it comes to issues of faith and love as God intended. Paul pleads with us to resist the works and words of the enemy by being *present* and not being frightened off. Paul invites us to use the power of God to set ourselves against

Satan's lies and destruction. When we stand in the presence and power of God, we have His authority—and what a mighty weapon that is! So if God's calling you to stand somewhere and to be a loving example of who He is, don't back down. You can stand in His presence and see Him work out His purposes. Isn't that fantastic?

When we stand in the presence of our strong and mighty God, He reminds us that who He is and what He does will never change. We can have absolute confidence that as we stand with Him, He's not going to suddenly move the goal posts, or disappoint us with a retreat strategy. God already won this battle against the enemy when Jesus defeated death by dying a sinless death on the cross and rose to life again. The enemy knows God's word is true, unchanging, and powerful. The enemy strategically distracts us from the truth of the Father's constancy and leads us to believe all kinds of nonsense! So, I (and forgive me for this old English word, but nothing fits better!) *beseech* you to stand on the truth, to stand in the presence of our Holy Father, and to stand on the facts of the Holy Spirit's discernment. Don't back down because *you don't need to*! God has already won and we get to stand up and resist the enemy's strategies from that place of victory.

And what kind of standing posture should we establish? Whilst doing some reading on the Internet recently, I stumbled upon this brilliant extract from "American Physical

Education Review" which was first published in 1916, and taken from a thesis presented by Thomas J. Browne in 1915. Read this in the context of how you "stand" as a believer in Jesus:

> The habit of a good posture is automatic; given certain stimuli, good posture will result. The sight of a soldier standing well will stimulate a boy to lift his head higher.
>
> Once formed, the habit tends to remain unchanged; the reaction occurs regardless of details and feelings. A trained West Pointer will not slouch even though feeling depressed or gloomy.
>
> Attention is minimized once the habit is established; there is not slouching when the mind is off guard. West Point cadets stand as well when standing about in conversational groups, as they do when on parade. The fatigue of holding oneself in good posture disappears with practice…
>
> The habit of good posture is specific; that is, one may walk well, yet not stand well or sit well.[1]

"The habit of a good posture…" As I write this, I'm sitting up straighter and remembering my ballet teacher telling us to think about a string going from our toes to the top of our head and all the way up to the sky! You can recognize a dancer from how she carries herself, from her posture, and how she stands. You can identify a soldier from the purposeful way he

walks and the strength in his stance. So here's my question: can others know you walk with Jesus and stand in a position of God-given, love-soaked authority? When others hear you talk or see how you respond to a personal crisis, do they have a sense that you won't sit down in the corner because you *stand* on the Truth?

As I said earlier, I have had to learn *how* to stand. And the truth is that I am still learning. I have intentionally built the "habit of good posture" in my thinking and reactions, which has allowed my natural responses ("regardless of details and feelings") to be that of standing on the truth. I can confidently hold my head high because I recognize God is in control and His word stands forever.

And what about this?

"...one may walk well, yet not stand well..."

Let's be the kind of people who run the race set before us (Hebrews 12:1) with kindness, deliberate love, and gentle obedience to God. Let's be those who walk with faith (2 Corinthians 5:7), steadily following the footsteps of our Lord. And let's be those who are able to stand well when the time comes. Remember, this is not an inactive, passive standing, but a mark of immovable resilience.

When the Father asks me to stand and see Him at work, or to stand up for truth, or to recognize that His word stands forever, I want to believe Him and obey immediately. I want that to be my *habit of good posture*.

God commands us to stand—and He also instructs us to *be still*. Stillness seems extraordinarily countercultural. Often when greeting people with, "How are you?" they respond with, "Oh, busy!" We pride ourselves on the fullness of our calendars and wear busyness like a badge of honor. Believe me, I understand how life can reach a frenetic pace. I speak with no condemnation, and I am preaching to myself. Let's rethink our hectic pace and make stillness our aim.

And here's why:

"Be still and know that I am God." (Psalm 46:10)

When we can find stillness, we can find God. Please hear me: I'm categorically not saying God cannot be found in the chaos and in the noise. He can show up wherever and whenever He likes, and He does. But our inner voice, the most inside part of us, needs to find stillness in order to hear God clearly.

Stillness is defined as "not moving or making a sound…quiet, calm, unmoving." Stillness is *surrender*. It is putting yourself in a position of quiet calm while focusing on the character of God. Quiet calm without focus is wasted stillness! God gives us the gift of stillness to put aside all the other "stuff" and focus on Him. If I am resolved to be unmoving on the inside, then in that still place I can see where God is moving instead of where I am doing all the moving. I absolutely believe that we can be still whilst running the children to ballet or swimming, whilst giving a crucial presentation to that big client or whilst attending the third doctor's appointment of the day. Being still is an act of the will and a constant state of being (which I am still learning!) with the help of the Holy Spirit.

> "The Lord will fight for you; you only need be still."
> (Exodus 14:14)

Our stillness creates space for God's glory to shine through our lives and our circumstances. So don't stand and fidget! Don't stand and anxiously look over your shoulder to see what God has overlooked. Don't stand and worry about *anything* because when you stand still in His presence, you're doing what God has asked you to do. And there can surely be nothing better.

While writing this song, God unfolded something that was not my original intent. I struggled with the placement of the punctuation—the unassuming comma or full stop can dramatically change the meaning of a phrase. They're quite feisty little things! The first line of the chorus (and, indeed, the title) could read, "Stand still in His presence." Or it could say, "Stand. Still. In His presence..." We talked a lot about it in the studio while we were recording and naming the file. As you can see, my preference was to use, "Stand. Still." because both words are individual and important actions. But the God of all creativity and poetry had more to say.

"Stand. Still in His presence." Did you get that? *Where* we stand is so very important. If I'm standing and being still, but not doing them in the presence of Father God, it's all wasted. There's such joy in the presence of God! Only there will we find the safety and majesty of our Creator, King, and Savior. Learning to rest constantly in His presence is a sure way of finding stillness (Exodus 33:14, Psalm 21:6, 1 John 4:16, Psalm 16:11). When the Spirit of God lives in us, we have the privilege of being perpetually in His presence (Psalm 139:7). No matter where we *stand*, we are *still* in His presence! May we be those who are both attentive and responsive to that honor.

Let the words of this song reach a tender place in your heart, and learn with me how to stand and how to be still. Commit with me to seek out those quiet spaces where we can abide in His presence and hear His voice. Only in that place can we find true peace in the midst of chaos.

Jesus, you promise us that You will never leave us and never forsake us (Hebrews 13:5). Please help us to be turning our hearts and our minds consciously towards You. Holy Spirit, how we need You to fill us up so that we are constantly being reminded of who we are in You and who You are in us. We need You to help us to let You do Your work. Teach us how to stand with a great posture of faith and how to be still in absolute confidence. We need You. We wait for You. Thank you that You will always accomplish Your plans.

Amen.

Two

Perfect Rest (Nate's Song)

The Song:

Verse 1:
Come to Jesus, you will find rest
He is waiting, you're an invited guest
It's liberating
He'll never let you go
You don't have to struggle on your own.
Come to Jesus, trust and obey
Let God hold you, submit to his way
He's your protection
He'll never let you go
You don't have to struggle on your own.

Chorus:
'Cause Jesus when I'm here, here in your presence
There's complete safety and I can let go
Release my burdens
And I know that as I draw near to you

Jesus you give the blessing of your rest
Your perfect rest.

Verse 2:
Come to Jesus, quietly wait
He is present here in this place
He is your refuge
He'll never let you go
You don't have to face today alone.
Come to Jesus, come now, today
Let God soothe you, don't be afraid
He's your provider
He'll never let you go
You don't have to face today alone.

Bridge:
And God says:
Child come to me
Child trust in me
Child rest in me
Child sit with me
Beloved (repeat bridge)

Final chorus:
'Cause Jesus when I'm here, here in your presence
There's complete healing and I can let go
Release my burdens

And I know that as I draw near to you
Jesus you give the blessing of your rest
Your perfect rest.

The Story: Perfect Rest (Nate's Song)

"Something's terribly wrong with Nathan!" Cindy was holding her precious 11 month old in her arms when he went completely limp. He was not responding. Thankfully the paramedics there at the Easter celebration in the park were on hand to help, and he was rushed to hospital. After initial treatments, he was quickly transferred to the children's hospital a few miles away. Nick and Cindy could only anxiously wait as the doctors did numerous tests on their tiny bundle of blond joy. The doctors finally came to them with a diagnosis. "We are sorry to tell you Nathan has cerebral palsy."

The words shattered what had been the silence of the unknown, exploding into their world with a crushing weight—which, unbeknownst to them, would only grow heavier in the coming days.

Nate endured more tests, as he continued to have multiple hourly seizures that turned him from a bouncy little boy into a floppy shell of himself. The doctors returned with a new diagnosis, thus beginning a new normal for their family.

"I'm afraid our initial diagnosis wasn't quite right. Nate does not have cerebral palsy. He has a leukodystrophy. The white matter in his brain is gradually disintegrating." The disease was scattered all over his brain, and no cure existed.

Suddenly, Cindy longed for the original diagnosis. This was much worse. This was unbearably finite. The caving roof of cerebral palsy at least seemed slightly recoverable and manageable, but the all-consuming fire of leukodystrophy was unquenchably devastating.

I didn't meet Cindy until Nate was 10. By that time, Nathan was confined to a wheelchair and had lost the ability to communicate. He received his nourishment through a feeding tube, and his family and other caregivers met all his needs. The love and assistance offered to Nate always astounded me. He was simply another member of their family of seven. He was Nate, and he was adored.

During his fifteenth year the inevitable happened, and Nate's health became even more unstable. Though he had a DNR order, he was admitted to hospital because his seizures were uncontrollable and he was utterly exhausted. Nick and Cindy sought medical intervention because their son had become "vacant," and they simply couldn't watch it happen any more. They spent a few long days in the pediatric hospital that was so familiar to them, and the doctors did their utmost to stop the dreadful onslaught of interruptions and dysfunction on Nate's body as he experienced hundreds of seizures. Cindy quietly expected to say their final goodbye to Nate during that hospital stay.

The doctors were able to halt the seizures with some very powerful medicine, so Nick and Cindy delightedly brought Nate home to the family. He was still very sick and was not responding to anyone. The aggressive attack of the seizures had utterly drained his tall, slim body of any remaining energy. The medicine had won the battle for peace whilst simultaneously removing his ability to fight. Nate seemed empty.

I had been in contact with Cindy during this time. When I learned that Nate was heading home, I texted her and offered to pray with them. But as I typed I heard the Holy Spirit whispering in my ear, *Sing over him, too. Sing "Come to Jesus."* I had written this song months earlier and had sung it in larger ministry settings, where it was well-received. But the thought of singing it over Nate felt awkward. Cindy and I had never really talked about faith, and she'd never heard me sing. Embarrassed and unsure of myself, I ignored that quiet voice and finished my text offering only to pray. However, as I went about my afternoon, cooking dinner and collecting the children from school, His voice became insistent. When an impression won't fade, I know God is speaking and I should listen.

Honestly, I took the easy way out. Instead of calling Cindy, I texted:

"I'm looking forward to coming over and praying with you over Nate. How would you feel if I brought my guitar and sang a song for him too? I wonder if it might disturb him because he's sleeping? I don't want to upset him. I know that Nick is working from home and I don't want to interrupt him either. I don't mind if you think that would be too much. I'll definitely come to pray though. xx"

Can you hear my resistance? I gave Cindy *every* opportunity to say no. But she swiftly and simply replied, "I'd love that."

I cannot adequately express my thankfulness for putting aside my pride and nerves that day and obeying what the Holy Spirit had called me to do—for what occurred in the family room of that cozy Texas home changed my life forever.

I arrived, guitar in hand and heart in anxious reliance on God, prepared to sing to Nathan and to pray healing over his weakened frame. As I greeted this teenager, who lay completely still on the sofa, Cindy reminded me he had not made any attempt at moving or even opening his eyes since he came home from the hospital. Their hope of seeing their Nathan again had evaporated.

Nate's tousled, blond hair lay carelessly against his pillow, and his long legs stretched to the end of the sofa. I explained what I was going to do and asked him to allow me to pray over him. As expected, he gave no response.

I began to sing, and I was struck again by the lyrics. "Come to Jesus, you will find rest." How apt! Nate had no other choice. He *had* to rest. And as I sang, I prayed. I asked God to show Nate how to rest *in Him*. I asked Jesus to reveal to Nate that he was forever held in the loving arms of our King. I asked the Father to allow Nathan to release his burdens to the only One able to completely take them away.

The atmosphere in the room was palpable. God began to reveal His presence to the three of us, though we could not have foreseen just how *deeply* He would make that presence known in the following seconds. As I sang, something in Nathan "loosened." I can't explain it any other way. All at once, Nate stretched out his arm towards my guitar, stared Cindy straight in the face and uttered a guttural sound of appreciation. That intensely unconscious teenager had returned to us from his place of empty immobility. God had worked a miracle! Cindy had no eyes for me; she was transfixed by the return of her precious boy. Nate took no notice of me either as he enjoyed his renewed ability to manipulate his arms, turn his head, and emit sounds. In that moment Nate did something he had not done for many, many years—he looked deeply into the eyes of his mother and connected his soul with hers. Yes, he was the same boy with the same needs and disabilities, but he was *back*, and that was the blissful truth.

The family soaked in another fourteen months with Nate until the Father healed him completely on Christmas Day 2014, bringing him home to heaven.

Nate was uniquely gifted. Yes, he was different, but his apparent deficits allowed him many unseen privileges. Nathan knew how to be still. Nate was acutely loved by his family and by many others. He never had concern for his physical or emotional needs because they were always carefully and lovingly met. He never needed to worry about anything, and his lack led him to a place of abundance. His "empty hands" left room for God to fill them. Cindy beautifully noted, "He was blessed because God was *in* him so much. He didn't have to deal with the chaos. He could feel and respond to God at any given moment." God genuinely lived inside Nate, and Nate knew it. Nathan realized his limitations and responded with superior stillness.

I want to be like Nate. I want his attitude of complete reliance upon God to be the way I approach Jesus every moment. As I sang to Nate that day, he seemed to experience the music and the God-connection in a concentrated place of intense intimacy. It was as if he crawled into the lap of Jesus, relaxed his head against the chest of his Lord, and welcomed that place of perfect rest.

I will never be the same. Nathan taught me the importance of responding in obedience to the quiet voice of God. He also showed me the simplicity of coming to Jesus in an act of tranquil reliance on a powerful God. I come to Him in quiet stillness, and He reveals His merciful and mighty presence. He bathes me in peace.

> "Come to Me, all who are weary and heavy-laden, and I will give you rest. Take My yoke upon you and learn from Me, for I am gentle and humble in heart, and you will find rest for your souls. For My yoke is easy and My burden is light." (Matthew 11:28-30 NASB)

Father God, as your children we long for deeper relationship with You. Teach us to be those who will run to You in all situations. May we be those who come to You willingly and often. Thank you that when we rest in You, we have complete safety and absolute freedom. We yearn for You, O God, come near as we draw close to You.

Amen.

Three

Shepherd King

The Song:

Verse 1:
You lead me by the side of quiet waters
And gently you restore my soul
I'll stay a while here in the greenest pastures
You satisfy
And you make me whole.

Chorus:
I'll always follow
Your tender guiding
Forever I'll be
Exalting and adoring you
My Shepherd King - Jesus

Verse 2:
And even when the cold of death's dark shadow
Prevents the warmth of sun on me

I fear no evil for your hand of mercy
It holds me for eternity.

(Chorus)

Bridge:
I'm welcomed to your feast
Your joyful strength released
So I can stand against my enemies
The torrent of your grace
Engulfs me in this place
I cannot help but worship you!

(Chorus)

The Story: Shepherd King

I crafted "Shepherd King" straight out of the well-known twenty-third Psalm. Because I felt like it was so familiar to me, I wanted to spend some more time with it to see what I had missed. Even when I think I know a verse or a passage of Scripture, I can always find something new or deeper when I spend fresh and concentrated time there.

God reminds us of His constancy in Psalm 23. Using the images of a Shepherd, the water and the grass, we can hear Father whispering of His unfailing nature of nurture.

A friend of mine is a shepherdess. She has missed many family gatherings and outings because of her commitment to her flock. Her job is to feed the sheep, put them in fresh pastures, tend the lambing mothers, and look after the helpless and sometimes orphaned lambs; their overall well-being was entrusted to her. Because she has spent time with them, they know her voice and are always delighted to see her.

Jesus called Himself our Shepherd (John 10:11). He cares for our immediate needs, He cares about our general, day-to-day existence, and He cares about our life-long needs. We can completely trust Him as our Shepherd, our leader, and our provider. God loves to meet our pressing needs and will hear us when we cry out in desperation for Him.

As a mother, my primary role involves meeting my children's needs. When they are infants, they cannot feed themselves, clean themselves, or comfort themselves. That is my job—but I cannot stop there. If I only ever met the physical needs of my children, they would be starved of love and compassion. In order to raise well-rounded people, I must do more than simply feed their stomachs. I must also feed their souls.

And it's the same for Jesus the Shepherd. He desires to *nurture* us and construct us into His image. He is always with us (Matthew 28:20), and therefore, we can always follow His leading. Always. When we spend time with Him we will know His voice (John 10:27) and be able to respond to Him when He calls. He is wholly committed to making us more like Him and bringing glory to Himself as we honor who He is.

The *Good* Shepherd will meet my needs and draw me into His love.

> **"He makes me lie down in green pastures. He leads me beside still waters. He restores my soul."**
> **(Psalm 23:2-3a)**

Consider water. The water in Psalm 23 is *quiet* water. The Hebrew word in this verse is *měnuwchah*, which can also mean "the rest of God." But even quiet, resting water does not remain motionless. It could be moving, unseen under the surface. Whether crashing, majestic waves or wandering, placid streams, water always elicits from us a profound response. The repetitive sound of movement and the assurance of its unending rhythm draws us deep into thought and contemplation. A receding tide will eventually come in. A dry river will in due time be replenished. And although the water may evaporate, it is still in its very essence, water. It is unchangeable and reliable.

Water reminds us God, too, is always moving but never changing. The way we relate to God may alter, but our God is constant. Perhaps my *feelings* about His closeness may vary, but the truth of His presence is unwavering. He is faithfully available for my refreshment and my cleansing (John 4:14, John 7:37-39).

Green pastures. Green. Healthy, ripe, well-nourished, and flourishing. In verse 2 of this Psalm, the grass is not turning yellow or brown. It's not unhealthy grass or grass entering a new season of change. It's *green* grass. This grass makes you want to kick off your shoes and experience its coolness around your toes. It is a safe and rich pasture, a place for flocks to feed, and then lie down and rest as the shepherd guards them.

This is where the Shepherd leads me; this place of great nourishment, quiet, and peace. In this pasture I can be certain of His protection and nurture. He leads me here so I can lie down and relax in His presence as He watches over me. This pasture is a place of consistent calm and stable stillness. Who knows what kind of chaos disrupts the town just over the hill? Right here, in this green pasture, there is holy harmony and tranquility.

We find this green pasture by allowing Jesus to lead us there. We must choose to lie down in the grass. Jesus will never force us to be still. He desires that we do, but it is not an obligation. And because He *leads* us there and doesn't *send* us there, we can be certain that He remains there with us and tends to us. He will bless us with His magnificent presence. All we have to do is eat, lie down, and rest. Like the *měnuwchah* of the water, this green, nourishing pasture allows me to simply enjoy the tranquil stillness of His presence, always.

Whilst this stillness needs to be an internal place of a quiet soul (as in the story for "Stand. Still."), I encourage you to physically find this kind of tranquility every day. You may have to create an official engagement on your calendar, but give yourself the gift of rest in a "green pasture," and allow the Shepherd to tend to you.

"Even though I walk through the valley of the shadow of death, I will fear no evil…" (Psalm 23:4a)

There will come a day for all of us where we feel overwhelmed with grief. Statistically, one out of every one person will die. We all have to stare into the face of sorrow at losing someone we love at some point.

There are always valleys among hills and mountains. It is geographically impossible to have places of raised land without lower land too. They have to exist beside each other. You can't have the top of a hill without also having the bottom of a hill. And so it is with life. We have days filled with joy and excitement that feel like standing on top of the world. We often describe these as "mountain top" experiences. But the rhythm of life dictates we will also have to walk through the low seasons of life, and they can feel like dark and unending valleys.

If, as you read this, you are experiencing the depth and darkness of a valley, remember there will be an end. There may be a climb ahead of you, but I promise you the climb is worth the effort.

If you have ever done any summer hiking, you know that on a hot, sunny day there is little more lovely than finding some constant shade to walk in. Just a little shelter from the beating sun provides much-needed refreshment and cooling. Conversely, if you've ever hiked on a cold day, there is nothing more lovely than emerging out of the shade and into the sun. The high sides of a valley afford you both of these experiences.

At some point in the day, the sun will shine down into the valley. And at some point in the day, the sun will *not* reach down into the valley. But you can guarantee the sun will shed light (even if from behind the clouds) into the depths of the valley for some portion of the day.

When we find ourselves in the cold darkness of a valley, when we feel empty and alone, the Shepherd reminds us in Psalm 23 that He is with us. His "rod and staff" are nearby to guide us because this Shepherd hasn't lost sight of us. He knows exactly where we are and where He wants to lead us. He is always present, whether in the valley or on the mountaintop.

I love what G.K. Chesterton said about valleys: "One sees great things from the valley, only small things from the peak."[2] Although a painfully beautiful reality, our Shepherd can teach us intricate truth about ourselves and about Him from the cold ground at the bottom of a valley. Don't miss what the Shepherd is teaching you from His position of close comfort. He is very near, and you are not alone. Allow Him to tenderly guide you, even here.

> **"You prepare a table before me in the presence of my enemies." (Psalm 23:5a)**

As I was writing this song, I had an image that helped me to see this Psalm in a different light.

Who are my enemies? Well, that is a big question! Perhaps you do have literal enemies, or maybe you don't experience a direct opposition from anyone. The Hebrew word here is *tsarar,* which obviously does translate as "enemy," but can also mean "distress," "bind up," "vex," "afflict," "besiege," among others.

When I began to think about people who "distress" me or make me feel inferior and "bound up," or those who have "afflicted" me in some way (and my response to them is admittedly *my* issue and not theirs!), I get a much clearer picture. There have been people who have opposed me, making my life difficult because of my faith in Jesus and the truth that I follow. So, yes, they are my "enemies."

However, we must remember that although our enemies sometimes appear to walk in human form, our true enemies are not of this world. Those who seemingly oppose us act out of a place of hurt or brokenness, and it is not us but the Jesus in us whom they are against. Ephesians 6:12 reminds us

> "…our struggle is not against flesh and blood, but against the rulers, against the authorities, against the powers of this dark world and against the spiritual forces of evil in the heavenly realms."

So imagine this: Those unseen, spiritual enemies revel in seeing me walk through the valley. They laugh at me as I wander in the darkness, far away from the top of the open gorge. My enemies see that I appear to be lost. Those forces who are against me delight in my low position beneath them, and they mock me from their position of apparent victory.

But they don't see the Shepherd walking beside me. They are too far away to witness how deeply in conversation He is with me. Their distant view from the top of the ledge prevents them from seeing the details I can see, and they are missing out! As I round the next bend in the valley, I come upon a table set with a gorgeous white tablecloth, candles, and flowers and absolutely *laden* with the most amazing food. This table is *enormous*. In fact, it's so big that those peering down from the side of the valley can clearly see what lies before me. But they are not invited to join me at this feast and will have to watch me enjoy it from their distant position. You see, I am in the company of the Shepherd, but they have chosen not to follow Him. This is a position of eternal victory, and my spiritual enemy witnesses the blessings of God even in that place.

I imagine this feast from my Shepherd will give me new sustenance and vigor before we climb out of the valley together. And when my Shepherd offers me the gift of refreshment and vindication, I have only one response: worship.

He is a good Shepherd who gives rest, who sustains us, and who loves to lift us up so that His name can be glorified. Rest with Him, trust in Him, and worship Him.

———————◇———————

Shepherd King, thank You that You always know exactly what I need. I praise You because You have promised that You will walk with me through every season of life. Teach me how to seek Your face in the apparent darkness and how to delight in Your presence as I feast on Your truth. Thank You that You are a good Shepherd who knows my name.
Amen.

Four

This Is Our Prayer

The Song:

Chorus:
This is our prayer, O Lord our God,
We long for you to move.
Hear now our prayers, O Lord our God,
Our hearts cry out to you.

Verse 1:
Abandoned hope, mystified hearts,
Families are wasting away.
We need your love, brandishing peace,
Equip us and send us today.

(Chorus)

Verse 2:
Nations are crushed, futures undone,
Identity's melting away.

We need your truth, brandishing joy,
Equip us and send us today.

(Chorus)

Verse 3:
Eternal God, conquering King
We're humbled before you today
You're able to move, you promise to save
Restoring your loved ones again.

(Last Chorus)
You hear our prayer, O Lord our God,
We're confident you will move.
You answer our prayers, O Lord our God,
Our hearts will trust in you.

The Story: This Is Our Prayer

Prayer is important. If you are a believer in Jesus, prayer should become as natural to you as breathing. Has anyone ever said to you, "No, there's nothing you can do to help. Just pray!" Yes, we should pray. But it's not, and never was, and never will be *just* praying. Prayer is a powerful and important weapon given by God to wield against the enemy. Prayer is an easily accessible and ever-present tool for speaking God's authority and seeing situations and people changed.

My prayer life is far from all that it should be. But I am learning to allow the Holy Spirit to stir within me so I can know how, when, and why I ought to pray. Prayer is so very important. Prayer is vital.

At its most basic form, prayer is simply talking to God, chatting with Him about anything. If you have ever cried out, "GOD!" in a moment of panic or fear, that is a prayer—and it's a good one! When we seek to be heard by God, that's a prayer. When we approach God with thanks, that's a prayer. You can pray on your own and God hears, or you can pray in a group and God hears.

There's something beautiful about approaching the King of the entire universe and telling Him how you feel.

Nothing compares to the freedom of conversing with your Father God in the privacy of your own mind at any time in the day or night. Whilst prayer is not "allowed" in school in the US, no one can actually stop prayer from happening. There are millions of students, teachers, and parents praying in schools every single day. They may be praying in the quiet of their minds, but God hears and He answers (Matthew 6:5-6).

We can pray out loud, alone. Somehow this kind of prayer increases our faith, as it did with David (Psalm 142:1). David desperately prayed out loud, and I've followed his example. In listening to my own voice proclaiming words of truth aloud, I remind myself who God is and who I am.

We can also pray out loud in groups. Matthew 18:19-20 says

> "Again I say to you, that if two of you agree on earth about anything that they may ask, it shall be done for them by My Father who is in heaven. For where two or three have gathered together in My name, I am there in their midst." (NASB)

I don't fully understand why such power in agreement exists, but I believe it does. God tells me that when I am His, I carry His full authority. So when there are many of us assembled to pray, and each one of us carries His remarkable authority, what a mighty army of faith we are (Mark 16:17-18, Romans 8:31-32, 1 Corinthians 15:57, 1 Peter 5:9).

I decided to write this song from the perspective of a gathering of people, "This is *our* prayer." Joining with others to pray can be an unforgettable experience. During times of prayer with others, I have experienced our great God deeply. He promises His presence when we gather in His name, and He has certainly shown Himself as a Mighty Father in times of gathered prayer.

When you are grappling with an issue in your life, isn't it good to know that others agree with your stance? Others' agreement with your actions and attitudes during prayer provides assurance of "heading in the right direction." Praying in agreement also reminds the enemy we are praying from a place of unity, righteousness, and power.

So *why* do we pray? First, we talk to God for the same reason we talk to anyone with whom we have a relationship. We talk to God because we want to! Any relationship compels us to engage in conversation and to spend time together. Prayer is a two-way dialogue. God will talk to us, too. He will respond when we offer Him space in our hearts and minds, and as we know Him more intimately, we will more clearly hear His response.

This song speaks of a specific reason for praying: bringing the vast needs of the world to God and asking Him to do something mighty. Some may call that intercessory prayer. God does not need my reminders of what's going on in the world, and neither does He need my direction. However, as I speak to Him about the mess and chaos, the pain and the dysfunction, I'm reminding myself what hurts me also hurts God. When His people—that is, everyone He created—are in pain, God aches too. God deeply desires every person on this earth to walk in His way and choose relationship with Him. That in itself would bring unity and peace.

We cry out to God, imploring Him to reveal answers and send solutions for all the mess we see around us, which is precisely what he asks us to do.

> "If my people, which are called by my name, shall humble themselves, and pray, and seek my face, and turn from their wicked ways; then will I hear from heaven, and will forgive their sin, and will heal their land." (2 Chronicles 7:14, KJV)

Whilst I would say God is not a God of formula, but a God of grace and mystery who longs to hear from His children, we cannot ignore the if/then of this Scripture. *If* we humble ourselves before God, pray, spend time intentionally looking to God and stop behaving like those who don't know

Jesus, *then* God will hear and heal our land. God wants our hearts to be rightly positioned as we come to Him.

As a parent, I understand this. If one of my children were to purposely run a stone down the side of the car, not apologize, and then ask me for $20, I would likely not respond very positively. There would need to be a change of heart and visible penitence before I would offer any kind of indulgence. (Even *with* an apology, I would need a significant cooling-off period before I could act with generosity!) And unlike God, I'm a flawed human being. But our Father wants us to come to Him, fully and humbly trusting Him and not ourselves, so He can generously heal us *as well as* healing the entire land. The Lord loves completion and wholeness. When we live in right standing with Him, we are able to seek right standing for others too. Matthew Henry, in his commentaries on Chronicles says, "Pardoning mercy makes ways for healing mercy."[3] Let us receive both His pardoning mercy and His healing mercy and live in the truth of it.

When we ask Father God to move within the situations and circumstances around us, He will answer. His replies often come in the form of obedient people whom He equips and sends in His name. We must be willing and available to be those who carry His answer.

I intentionally wrote the verses of this song in two halves. The first half asks God to bring about necessary change, and the second half asks God to show us how He wants to use us in that change. God freely provides the "weapons" we need by equipping us with the fruits of the Spirit. Galatians 5:22-23 says

> "…the fruit of the Spirit is love, joy, peace, forbearance, kindness, goodness, faithfulness, gentleness and self-control. Against such things there is no law."

Consider the last phrase of these verses: "Against such things there is no law." What a brilliant provision for the Father to bless us with "weapons" that can never be illegal! Let us never forget they are fully available to us, and let us always seek to wield them.

We cannot forget Ephesians 6:12, which reminds us

> "…our struggle is not against flesh and blood, but against the rulers, against the authorities, against the powers of this dark world and against the spiritual forces of evil in the heavenly realms."

The battles we wage with prayer should focus on the root of the problems. The origin of all hostility is surely spiritual. We must remember we are contending within the heavenly realms, and as we do so, we show the fruit of the Spirit in its fullness towards those whom we face. Watchman

Nee puts it this way, "We must have a spirit of power towards the enemy, a spirit of love towards man, and a spirit of self-control towards ourselves."[4]

Our loving responses can never be underestimated. A ripple effect occurs when we love and honor those around us. Yes, we *must* pray for God to reach those so terribly wounded and desolate around the world, and we can ask the Lord to equip our spiritual brothers and sisters who live in those communities. But equally, we must stand ready to be part of the solution to the problems much closer to home, and indeed, on our doorstep.

When we cry out to God in desperation, He hears us, and we can be one hundred percent certain He will answer. We can audaciously end any prayer, whatever that prayer is, by thanking God for hearing us and trusting He will powerfully move.

God deserves our trust because He never fails. The God who has called us to serve Him, the God who loves us so freely, the God who is ever-present holds the keys to revelatory resolutions, and He gladly chooses to use us in the process. Thank you, God!

———————⋄———————

Living, loving God, we are pained by the hurt, fear and devastation that we see in Your world. We acknowledge that without You, there is no hope. We are so deeply grateful that with You there is not only hope but also freedom and joy. Teach us to carry the "weapons" of love, joy, peace, patience, kindness, goodness, faithfulness, gentleness and self-control. We offer ourselves freely to You for You to use as instruments of Your solutions. We love You and are so grateful for Your faithfulness. Thank You for hearing us and answering our prayers.

Amen.

Five

Devotion

The Song:

Chorus 1:
Unchanging
Unceasing
Unblemished God
I will worship you
All loving
All knowing
All caring God
I will worship you

Verse 1:
And I'm in awe of who you are
And I'm amazed at how you save
Yes I will worship you

Chorus 2:
Unfailing
Unending
Uncreated God
I will worship you
All powerful
All holy
All victorious God
I will worship you

Verse 2:
And I will wonder at your ways
And I will marvel at your grace
Yes I will worship you

Bridge:
I am compelled to bring praise
With every breath you have made
You are the King of my life
I will worship you
And everything that I do
Will be my love gift to you
For my devotion is yours
I will worship you

Bridge 2:
There is no one like you
There is no one like you
Jesus, King of kings
And Lord of lords
Above all else

The Story: Devotion

When I'm settling down to worship Jesus, I love to think about all that He is. It is a very, very long list! It's fun to search the Internet for a list such as, "Bible verses about who God is," or "Bible verses about who Jesus is," or "What does the Bible say about the Holy Spirit?" Go ahead—try it for yourself, and you'll find extensive lists of Scriptures that point to who God, Jesus and the Holy Spirit are. Go on, put this book down and go and see exactly who we worship. I promise that reading Scripture will benefit you and feed your soul way more than anything I can say here! (Pause for reader to search the Scriptures…)

So now that you've read WHO our God is in the Bible, which is the ultimate truth, let's talk about how I came to write "My Devotion." (And to those of you who didn't do that yet, it's ok, you can do that now instead… Go on!)

One day, I was thinking deeply about the many facets of Jesus' nature, and I sat down with my guitar and my Internet search to remind God who He is. Now, you may think that's a rather arrogant and unnecessary exercise—surely God doesn't need to be reminded who He is? Right! That's very true. God never needs my reminder about who He is because He is absolutely settled in that truth already. Hebrews 13:8 says

"Jesus Christ is the same yesterday, today and forever."

And Psalm 18:30a tells us

"This God—His way is perfect; the word of the Lord proves true…" (ESV)

Also, Numbers 23:19 states

"God is not human, that he should lie, not a human being, that he should change his mind. Does he speak and then not act? Does he promise and not fulfill?"

So, why on Earth did I feel the need to remind God who He is?

I love singing songs about who God is *to me*, and I love to sing and thank Him for all He's *done*. It's wonderful to be able to express in music how much *I* love Him, but *newsflash Tedford*, it's not all about you! How the Lord has blessed me, and healed me, and helped me, how much I love Him—all those thoughts are relevant and important. But, on that day, I just needed to express the simple facts of exactly who He is.

There's great power in speaking out loud who our Father is. When I breathe life into the pages of Scripture by putting an actual voice to them (rather than just reading them in my head), I am not only declaring truth to my own ears and heart, but to the ears and heart of the universe. The Scripture is littered with hundreds of verses telling us to sing our praise and adoration to our heavenly King. It's not something new, and it's clearly important enough to merit about 400 references in the Bible. And interestingly the Bible tells us to sing about God both to *Him* and to *one another*, connecting us to both.

There's also an often-unseen level of spiritual warfare going on when we sing out exactly who God is. Revelation 12:11 says

> "And they overcame him because of the blood of the Lamb and because of the **word of their testimony**, and they did not love their life even when faced with death." (Emphasis mine, NASB)

We can overcome the enemy by what comes out of our mouths. So let it be praise! Allow it to be worship! Encourage yourself to speak and sing out the truth of who our marvelous God is!

Hebrews 2:12 (with a reflection back to Psalm 22:22) shows us that Jesus also sings in the gathering of people who have come to worship God. So, if it's good enough for Jesus…! Matthew Henry, in his commentary on Hebrews, says "…Christ would sing praise to his Father in the church. The glory of the Father was what Christ had in his eye; his heart was set upon it, he laid out himself for it, and he would have his people to join with him in it." Isn't that beautiful? Christ's eyes and heart were fixed on praising His Father and reminding those around Him to do the same. So let us be obedient to that call.

When writing the lyrics to "My Devotion," I decided to use the prefix *un-* to counter our culture's view to the way that current culture sees each member of the Trinity. Many believe God is not quite enough, or that Jesus is outdated, or that the Holy Spirit was only meant for ancient times. I am deeply saddened when I hear people talk about how God failed them and how He cannot possibly be a perfect god. With the simple addition of those two little letters, we can sing out the truth that God is *un*failing, *un*blemished, and *un*ceasing in every way. We can sing this to Him and to each other as a reminder that when it seems like all is lost, God is *not* lost and is absolutely available and dependable.

We sing that He is all-powerful, all-loving, all-knowing, all-caring—each fantastically formidable truths. The addition of that small prefix *all-* makes these Biblical facts even stronger, reiterating the fact that God's completeness can never be revoked.

When singing these realities I am unquestionably compelled to respond with worship and devotion. I simply have to reply to those statements with honor, adoration, and reverence for my Great God. My desire is that as you sing those words, you too will be called to respond with your eyes and your heart fixed on the One to whom all praise is due. May you find your resting place—a life of devotion.

Father, Son and Holy Spirit, thank You that You make Yourself known to us. Thank You that as we get to know You more, there will always be a new facet of Your brilliant character we haven't fully grasped yet. Teach us to be the kind of people who continue to seek more of You. May we be grateful seekers of the Truth who are filled with decisive devotion as we choose to live our lives in You. We are compelled to bring You praise and bring our lives, our love gift to You.

Amen.

Six

In The Secret of The Stable

The Song:

Verse 1:
In the secret of a stable
Underneath the shining star
The King of all creation
Breathed the air.
In those meagre, dark surroundings
That Majestic baby knew
The time had come
To trample on despair!

Chorus 1:
So, draw me from the wonder of the stable
Take me to that cross upon the hill
Lead me to the victory of the empty tomb
And teach me how to live my life in you.

Verse 2:
This tiny baby Jesus
Drew worship from the wise
And honour from the lowliest of man.
They knelt before his brightness
And uttered words of praise
But staying here alone
Is not His plan.

(Chorus 1)

Verse 3:
In the wake of crucifixion
Wrapped in mourning and distress
They came to worship Jesus
One last time.
But they found His tomb was empty
He has beaten sin and death
He is reigning, He has conquered, He's alive!

(Chorus 1)

Chorus 2:
I kneel before this King who came to save us
I offer Him the worship of my heart
My voice will join with millions of his children
We glorify God's Son who rescued us!
We glorify God's Son who rescued us!

The Story: In The Secret of the Stable

I love Christmas. There are years of memories and stories tucked away in that dust-covered Christmas box that comes down from the attic every year. There are cut-out paper snowflakes and chunky reindeer with wonky antlers that hold a special place in my heart. Somehow, I have ended up with the Christmas Angel from my childhood tree. She never makes it to the top of the tree these days due to her disheveled appearance, but I love to greet her smiling face and tousled hair each year as I think back to chilly Christmas nights in England.

Even if you don't celebrate with family traditions, most people love the lights and the warm-hearted feeling Christmastime brings. There's a general sense of kindness around, and we can enjoy the happy anticipation of children as they wait for Christmas morning.

Christmas Eve is one of the days in the year where many churches are most full. Communities come together to sing Christmas carols as part of their family tradition and to offer worship to the baby Jesus. A gentle voice reads the Christmas story, reminding us of how the narrative unfolds. We acknowledge each other with sincere joy and leave without another thought.

Joining together in a spirit of unity on Christmas Eve is nothing but good. Meandering through these traditions of joy and comfort is important and foundational. Repeating the truth in the Christmas story is vital and unmissable.

But, there is more…

If this one evening, indeed, this one season, doesn't move you to action, then its purpose has failed. The Christmas remembrance season should lead us to Jesus.

Jesus was a helpless baby. A child. He relied on His mother in the same way that each of us did. The neighborhood grannies would have admired baby Jesus and his cute smile or chubby cheeks in the age-old way that grannies have marveled at all babies. His coming was remarkable because it was ordinary.

Although not so ordinary when a whole host of heavenly beings sing you a "happy birthday" song! Not so ordinary when a group of wise astronomers travel for months in search of your very own star! Not so ordinary when the lowest of the low join the most sagacious and journey to the foot of your crib to bow down and worship!

But if we celebrate the birth of Jesus as a singular event and leave it there, then we have missed the point of the Gospel.

Because there is more…

Our daughter was born with the umbilical chord wrapped tightly around her neck. She was blue—and quiet. In those five…six…seven seconds of waiting, every remaining particle of strength I had after the birth process funneled into desperate prayers. The midwife calmly and proficiently held our newest treasure. With the confidence of one who had seen this before, she laid our strangely soundless child on my chest and told me to rub her and hold her close. As I beseeched the Lord to breathe His breath into her lungs, I stroked my baby's back and embraced her tiny form. She tilted her head back and as she opened her mouth she filled herself with the unfamiliar essence of life. Our brand-new human saturated the room with a cry of confidence as she sealed her arrival with the song of the newborn.

That was fifteen years ago. I will never forget how God answered our desperation with a moment of Creative Breath. But, that's not *who* our daughter is.

For there is more…

If you ask me about our daughter, I would tell you about how she didn't grow hair until she was two. How she broke her leg on a trampoline and earned the nickname "Bubbles" whilst in hospital in traction, due to her obsession with playing with bubbles. I would recount to you her first day at school and how her mummy cried as she left her in the classroom. Ask me *who* she is and I'll tell you she's a young lady who loves Jesus. A girl with Irish eyes and a twinkle of mischief. A whiz in the kitchen who bakes wickedly amazing cakes. I would tell you that she's smarter than I know how to be and more beautiful than any child I ever thought I'd have.

And yet, there's still more…

I cannot expect you to know all there is about my daughter from one or two paragraphs. Nor can I imagine that you would know who she really is just from the recounting of her remarkable birth story. Will I remember her birth? Oh yes! It's tattooed on my mind; the invading fear of those first delicate seconds will stay with me forever. But she is more than that moment. I have countless memories and celebrations tucked away in my mind that have created my connection with our daughter.

Because she is more.

And that is my point and what led me to write the song, "In the Secret of the Stable." If we only celebrate the birth of Jesus and leave it at that, we have missed so much of who Jesus is. If we only kneel in honest adoration of this baby King, we are overlooking the truth of the power displayed in His life. If we only bring gifts to the child Majesty, we are omitting the horrible necessity of His sinless death. If we only enjoy those gathering around the manger in the stable, we miss the exuberant joy of those who gathered around the empty tomb.

Jesus is more!

Yes, He was a baby, and let us always celebrate and gather to remember that reality. But He was also a man. A man who performed miracles. A man who walked on earth and around whom people gathered to hear His wisdom. Jesus was the man-God who chose to take our sin upon Himself and to release us from its enslaving power. Jesus was more than a baby. He was the man-Deity who wrestled death to the mat and returned victorious as the risen King.

Let us not miss that Jesus is more!

Never stop kneeling at the side of the manger and worshipping the baby. But don't stay there. Be one who is moved to grow in relationship with this tiny baby Jesus. Be one who is searching to find out *who* Jesus is. Let's be those who listen to His truth and allow Him to change us. We can be those who kneel at the foot of the cross and gaze upon our Lord as He chose to bring full redemption for those who love Him. Don't miss out on the exhilarating excitement of the risen Jesus. Allow yourself to be enraptured not only with the exhilarating excitement of the risen Jesus, but also with the bountiful blessing of the Holy Spirit.

So much more!

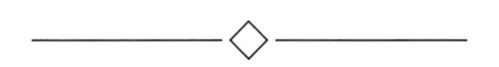

———————◇———————

Living King, Thank You for all that You are. Thank You that You not only came, but that You stayed and completed all that was ahead of You. Thank You that we are invited to kneel at Your feet and worship You. Thank You that You rescued us and that we get to be a part of Your eternal family. Thank You that You are more than we can really know. There will always be more until we see You face to face, and what a joy that will be.
Amen.

Seven

Father of All Days

The Song:

Verse 1:
I will not be ashamed
I'll proclaim you are Lord
Jesus you have captivated me
Saviour I am released

Chorus:
Father of all days
I will put my trust in you
Strong and loving King
I will bow to you alone
Ever reigning Lord
Lifted high through sacrifice
God who loves the world
I will live to bring you glory

Verse 2:
I'll be strong in your truth
Living life without fear
Spirit you pour boldness out on me
Use my life for your fame

(Chorus)

Bridge:
You're peace in life's crazy storms
You're rain when dry ground is parched
You're home for the heart without rest
Jesus, you're all this ruptured world needs

(Chorus)

The Story: Father of All Days

Sometimes I feel like there are gaps in what we sing about as the Church. One of the themes that seem to be missing is that of persecution. The word "persecution" is a word that conjures up all kinds of images. Many of us who have never faced death because of our faith (being killed for our faith is the ultimate persecusion) may actually agree we have seen a *level* of persecution. Perhaps you are a teacher and have found yourself to be constrained from talking about your relationship with Jesus to a student who is searching for something more. Maybe you have been told to stop talking about Jesus in an office environment because others in your team find His name to be offensive. I'm willing to bet that you have your own story to put in here that tells of a time where your love for Jesus led to a hostile response and maybe even ill treatment.

Jesus tells us

"In this world you will have trouble. But take heart! I have overcome the world" (John 16:33b).

And again in Matthew 5:11, Jesus says

"Blessed are you when people insult you, persecute you and falsely say all kinds of evil against you because of me."

Notice the two words "will" and "when." We are to *expect* people to come against us because of our religious beliefs. We should be *presuming* that because we demonstrate faith in the one true God, we will face opposition.

But, even if we are physically alone when these things happen, we are never truly alone because we are a part of the family of God.

When we gather to worship our Father, we sing. One of the benefits of singing together is that we, in part, are singing to each other. As we raise our voices in praise of our great King, we also remind each other of His worth and power. The words of "Father of All Days" are directed straight to God. It's a song where we get to address our Father whilst at the same time making a firm decision, ahead of time, about how we will choose to react and respond when we face persecution.

When I was penning this song, I imagined this to be my "declaration of dependence." It is an announcement to myself that I will be prepared to act out of a place of freedom in Jesus. It is my reminder to myself that I have pre-decided to live without the fear of other people's thoughts, opinions, and actions, but instead to be bold and loving as I declare the unchanging truth of who Jesus is. It is my proclamation to myself to remain in a state of mind that thoroughly depends on God.

The phrase "father of all days" formed in my thoughts after I read Deuteronomy 32.

> "Remember the days of old; consider the years of many generations; ask your father, and he will show you, your elders, and they will tell you. When the Most High gave to the nations their inheritance, when he divided mankind, he fixed the borders of the peoples according to the number of the sons of God." (v. 7-8, ESV)

God was my Father long before I acknowledged that fact. He will be my Father tomorrow. He will be my Father for the rest of the year and indeed for the rest of my eternity. All my days belong to Him (Psalm 139:16) whether those days are filled with joy or sorrow. He is the Father of every one of the days He has ordained for me. And that's a very safe and comforting place to be. No matter how my days turn out, I can be absolutely assured that the creator of the whole universe is my *Father!* Isn't that simply amazing?

Not only that, but He's also our Savior, our King, our Lord. He's God the Father, Jesus our brother, and Holy Spirit our helper. He is full of power and abounding in gentleness and love. He's saved and released us from the binding chains of sin and yet we choose to be bound and captivated by His greatness.

I love dichotomous words and phrases that describe our unique and multifaceted God. He is a strong King, yet He is also close and loving like a brother. He is merciful *and* mighty. Jesus paid our debt by dying for us, and yet He was also lifted high as the ultimate conqueror.

Our Messiah can also be described with phrases that bring a beautiful resolve. He is peace in our storms, He is rain in the drought, and He is home for the wanderer. He is all we will ever need.

Perhaps my meandering thoughts seem far from the subject of persecution, which is where we began this story. But it is precisely because of *who* our God is that we can face persecution with bravery and certainty. These two thoughts are opposite sides of the same coin; they belong together.

Let's be a people who encourage each other to intentionally *stand* for Jesus in the most difficult of situations. Let's be those who declare the solid truth of who our Father is, and let's be a harmonious, resonating orchestra of unified, beautiful sound as we remind the world around us that God is available to all.

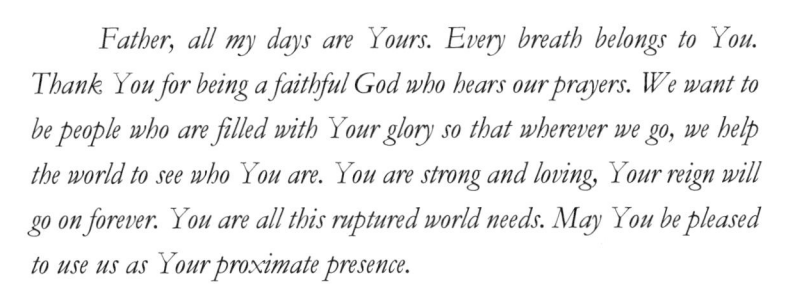

Father, all my days are Yours. Every breath belongs to You. Thank You for being a faithful God who hears our prayers. We want to be people who are filled with Your glory so that wherever we go, we help the world to see who You are. You are strong and loving, Your reign will go on forever. You are all this ruptured world needs. May You be pleased to use us as Your proximate presence.

Amen.

Eight

The Power of a Prayer
(for our Miri Moo)

The Song:

Chorus 1:
I believe in the power of a prayer
I have seen the answers God declares
He has heard each cry for healing
Every call for help and calm
I believe in the power of a prayer

Verse 1:
You do not walk alone
God is always moving
Keep your eyes focused on Him
And be always listening
Bring Him your praises
Bring Him your requests
Boldly come, to the throne of the King

Chorus 2:
I believe in the power of a prayer
I have seen the answers God declares
He has heard each cry for freedom
Every call for peace and strength
I believe in the power of a prayer

Verse 2:
Ceaselessly pray, you will see
God will move in power
Doing immeasurably more
Than you could imagine
Bring Him your worship
Bring Him your concerns
Boldly come, to the throne of the King

Chorus 3:
I believe in the power of a prayer
I have seen the answers God declares
He has heard each cry for wisdom
Every call for hope and life
I believe, I believe

Bridge:
So go ahead and pray the prayer
You think you can't believe
When you doubt that God can do the things

That seems so out of reach
Even if your faith's as small and quiet
As a whispered breath
Go ahead, pray the prayer

(Chorus 1)

Vamp:
Oh, I believe
I believe in the name of Jesus
Oh, I believe
I believe He can make me whole
Oh, I believe
I believe He can turn me around
Oh, I believe
I believe He can set the captives free
Oh, I believe
I believe in the healing power
Oh, I believe
I believe, I believe, I believe
Oh, I believe
I believe in the power of prayer
Oh, oh, oh, I believe
I believe, I believe
(I believe in the power of a prayer)
So go ahead pray your prayer.

The Story: The Power of a Prayer

This song was commissioned for the naming ceremony (or Baby Dedication) of our Goddaughter, Miriam Ruth.

Kirsty was devastated. Not one, but two doctors had now confirmed she would never again conceive a baby and give birth to another child. The son she and Danny already had was to be the first and last healthy child born to them. This news confused Kirsty because she had strongly felt the Lord impress on her heart that they would give birth to another baby. After two traumatic miscarriages, all the doctors' investigations confirmed Kirsty was no longer able to conceive on her own. After much deliberation Danny and Kirsty decided not to pursue the processes and disappointments surrounding IVF. They'd explored the possibility of adoption, but so many enormous and unsolvable obstructions made every hope quickly fade.

In her sadness, Kirsty came to God and told Him exactly how she felt about the diagnosis given by the medical professionals. In her bewilderment she cried out to the Father as she questioned her own ability to hear Him at all. In her turmoil she turned her heart directly towards the King of creation and begged Him to find another way.

At this point there was (and always is) a real need for the family of God to gather around and bring support and encouragement. Kirsty and Danny intentionally asked for specific help from a chosen group of people whom they trusted. It's not easy being the one who openly talks about the hard stuff. Too many people find this topic of conversation unacceptable and awkward and not something we need to discuss in polite company. Can we just take a moment to agree to be those who are willing to go to those places of the hard stuff, and to offer a hand of love and friendship to those who may be stuck there? For Danny and Kirsty, they found precious community willing to be very close and very present. These friends brought food, they cared for their son, and they listened without judging the flow of angry tears. Added to all of this was the most important help: they prayed.

Kirsty and Danny had prayed on their own, a most natural and obvious thing for them to do. But then they joined together to see this specific promise from God come to fruition—a battle against the diagnosis, whose victory would release the truth of healing and new life.

And so, we prayed. We prayed alone, we prayed in twos and threes, and we prayed in large groups. We held Kirsty's hand and prayed, and we prayed from the other side of the world. We prayed with intensity and intentionality, and we prayed briefly while sitting at a red light. We kept reminding our loving God of His promise, and we weren't going to stop until we knew He had heard us.

Then one day, my husband and I sat at our dinner table in Texas with my laptop open, answering a video chat with the two of them wearing sheepish grins, sitting in their living room in England. With excited and puzzled pauses, they falteringly told us they were pregnant! Our giggles of excitement quickly turned to tears of delight as we celebrated the beginning of a new journey that would be wrapped in many protective layers of prayer.

Her pregnancy was not easy, and many days we reminded God again and again of what He'd promised (Isaiah 43:26a)[i] and what He'd started. But our precious little Miriam (meaning "longed-for child") Ruth arrived a healthy, happy, wriggly little girl, and we celebrated with shouts of joy and more tears! We call her "Miracle Miri."

Like initials carved into a tree trunk, which grow with the tree, the night I sang over Miri at her baby dedication is beautifully etched into the trunk of my memory. With every year, every challenge, every flicker of doubt, her story grows more magnificent than its original design. If I ever need a marker to remind me how God answers the big prayers, I can sidle up to that tree and see her initials carved there. God does answer prayer. I have evidence to show you He does, and that evidence grows bigger and stronger every day.

On that cold Sunday evening, in a warm, packed church in an English village, full of grateful and harmoniously delighted faces, I sang the truth that "I believe in the power of a prayer." I believe because I have seen.

Sitting amongst those smiling faces was Maria, who had left her desperately ill husband at home. Peter was too unwell to come to church that evening. He was a great man who loved God and had served Him well. And Maria had prayed too. Alone, and on her knees, filled with faith, reminding God that He is able to heal. She had prayed with her daughters and her friends. Many, many people had prayed with deep certainty that God would bring Peter healing, and they had gathered in community around them. And yes, God healed Peter, but not in the way we had all hoped. God healed Peter by bringing him home to Heaven where he celebrates today, rejoicing in his perfectly whole body and singing with his uniquely beautiful bass tones to his Father.

Richard and Carolyn were also there that night, holding their own miracle, a new little girl named Beth (which means, "Our God is abundant"). Theirs was also a long and arduous journey with many visits to doctors and clinics and aching disappointments again and again. They had prayed and waited for almost six years. They had been petitioning the Father over and over again asking for this blessing to be theirs. And on this day their faces were filled with joyful gratitude as their arms held the fulfillment of His gift. God had never overlooked their tears (Psalm 56:8)[ii], and on this day their tears of delightful wonder powerfully reminded them He never forgets us. For this family of three, a new battle awaited them, which none of us knew on that day. But they were able to approach the next battle in the full knowledge that our Father hears and answers. They had a pot full of tangible truth into which they repeatedly immersed themselves during the next trial.

Ask Miri's parents if they believe in the power of a prayer.
Ask Peter's wife and children if they believe in the power of a prayer.
Ask Beth's mum and dad if they believe in the power of a prayer.

Each will answer with a resounding and thunderous YES! Regardless of the outcome, they will all say "yes." Regardless of whether the answer came in the way they wanted, they will say "yes." They have seen the power released with prayer. They proficiently reiterate their requests to God (1 Thessalonians 5:16-18)[iii]. They will tell you, probably through grateful tears, that the Lord hears, and the Lord answers. They will tell you to go ahead and pray your prayer, even if you can't fully believe it yourself (Matthew 17:20)[iv]. They will tell you to take your eyes off the circumstances yelling at you and demanding your attention, and to turn your eyes to gaze on the beautiful goodness of our Lord (Hebrews 12:2)[v]. They will tell you that miracles happen today.

They will tell you to pray.

In fact, if you met any of these people, they wouldn't just tell you to pray. I have no doubt they would *join* you in prayer. When we've seen our Father work in the depths of our own despair, when we've experienced Him pulling us out of the pit of anguish, then we have more faith to pray for others who are still there (2 Corinthians 1:4)[vi]. Nothing is out of the Father's reach; no one is beyond His grasp.

With courage or uncertainty, with boldness or desperation, with faith of any size—"go ahead, pray your prayer."

———◇———

Creator God, we are so grateful You hear us when we pray. You promise us in Your Word (Hebrews 4:16)[vii] we can come to You as Your children with boldness and in total confidence. We are deeply thankful You don't turn us away but instead You turn us towards You. Today we bring You our deepest needs. We dare to pray about the situation that seems hopeless to us. Nothing is ever hopeless to You, Father. Please move and work in that situation in new and fresh ways. Show us who You are and reveal more of Your miracle working power in that situation. We honor You, God. We adore You. We thank You in advance for the way that You have answered.

Amen.

ⁱ "Review the past for me, let us argue the matter together."

ⁱⁱ "Record my misery; list my tears on your scroll—are they not in your record?"

ⁱⁱⁱ "Rejoice always, pray continually, give thanks in all circumstances; for this is God's will for you in Christ Jesus."

^{iv} "He replied, "Because you have so little faith. Truly I tell you, if you have faith as small as a mustard seed, you can say to this mountain, 'Move from here to there,' and it will move. Nothing will be impossible for you." "

^v "…fixing our eyes on Jesus, the pioneer and perfecter of faith. For the joy set before him he endured the cross, scorning its shame, and sat down at the right hand of the throne of God."

^{vi} "…who comforts us in all our troubles, so that we can comfort those in any trouble with the comfort we ourselves receive from God."

^{vii} "Let us then approach God's throne of grace with confidence, so that we may receive mercy and find grace to help us in our time of need."

Nine

Perfecter of Our Faith

The Song:

Verse 1:
I will teach my soul to need you
In the same way that my lungs cry out for breath
I'll remind you of the mercy
That flows for us and reaches to the depths
My life be His reflection
My words and actions draw you nearer still
So you'll be free to be His mouthpiece
As you press on, solely focused on His will.

Verse 2:
I will urge my heart to love you
In every scene that life will have us play
I'll tell you He is gracious
And I will do my best to be the same
I know that God's been patient
And lavished me with more than I deserve

So I'll spend time searching deeply
Until each part of all you are is learned

Chorus:
And together we'll run
Together we'll move
Hand in hand we'll grow
And be much more of His love
Together in Him
Fixed on His gaze
The author of our union
The Perfecter of our faith

Verse 3:
I will point you to the Father
For He alone can meet your deepest needs
I will worship here beside you
Honour and adore Him on our knees
I will turn your face towards Him
So Jesus is the centre of your days
And in unity we'll seek Him
A partnership that forever brings Him praise

The Story: The Perfecter of Our Faith

I was honored to write this wedding song for our lovely friends, Jon and Jordan. May you both walk in the protection of a marriage covered by the love of our Heavenly Father. I can only write about marriage from my observations, and so this song was born out of my experiences.

> "Therefore, since we are surrounded by such a great cloud of witnesses, let us throw off everything that hinders and the sin that so easily entangles, and let us run with perseverance the race marked out for us. Let us fix our eyes on Jesus, the author and perfecter of our faith, who for the joy set before him endured the cross, scorning its shame, and sat down at the right hand of the throne of God. Consider him who endured such opposition from sinful men, so that you will not grow weary and lose heart." (Hebrews 12:1-3)

This year will mark twenty-one years of marriage to my amazing husband, Gareth. We met about three years before we got married. I asked him out for coffee (yes, I did!). He accepted my invitation, and the rest, as they say, is history.

Every day of our journey has been an adventure: challenging, thrilling, exhausting, exhilarating. Don't ever let anyone tell you that marriage is easy. It's not. And I've realized it's not meant to be easy. We have experienced gigantic celebrations and immense pain. We have lived days of fantastic fun and days of habitual normality. We have even faced moments of questioning and confusion. But the Master's Hand of steady confidence upheld us through all of it.

On the day that we said, "I do," we said those words both to each other and to the Father. We both knew and loved the Lord and were willing to surrender our plans to His. These last tewnty-one years have seen us run both our individual races as well as our joint race together.

When we were first married, we lived near one of the Royal parks in England. We loved to go there and walk and talk. But Gareth also loves to run long distances. I have never been a long distance runner (why do people do that?), so we came up with a creative way that we could do this together. I bought a pair of roller skates so that Gareth could run and I could skate along beside him. I had never skated before, and so the first day was a hilarious combination of solemn concentration and unreserved guffawing! We must have been quite a sight as Gareth held my hand and encouraged me to push forward and not be afraid. I was giggling and sucking in air, trying my best not to make a fool of myself in front of this new love of mine. A few weeks in, I inevitably fell. I had managed to find my rhythm and gain some speed when I accidentally skated over a small stone. It put a rapid stop to my forward momentum, and I found myself flat on my face, nursing a very painful wrist. Gareth caught up and helped me to my feet. After a long wait in the ER and an x-ray, I left the hospital heavily bandaged with torn ligaments, but thankfully no break. I had great fun the next day with my class of seven and eight year olds. Oh, the stories I told, from shark attack to pigeon invasion! But when I finally told them the truth, I earned considerable "cool" points for being out on skates!

Marriage is hard, and marriage is fun. Marriage is a race, a marathon. Just like my own faith walk (or skate!), marriage is a journey of discovery: of who I am in Jesus, who my spouse is in Jesus, and who we are together in Jesus.

Whilst I was learning to skate, Gareth held my hand, waited for me, encouraged me, and let me go even as I fearfully and unconfidently wobbled. Then he helped me up when I eventually fell. During my first slow days, he would run ahead of me to actually get the exercise he needed and then circle back around and run next to me.

When I was more proficient, I could skate faster than he could run, so then I would head off into the distance and come back to meet him where he was. Later I would skate just ahead of him, challenging him to push himself harder. In this process he obtained a faster and more consistent pace. Then, while I recovered from my injury, Gareth still ran on his own so that he could retain his fitness levels while I rested.

And this illustrates our journey of marriage.

As we got to know each other more, we realized we weren't always running our race of faith at the same pace. There have been times when Gareth has been running towards God, full steam ahead, and I've been a little slow to catch up. In these seasons, Gareth has blessed me by being Jesus to me. He has encouraged me to "get my skates on" and run alongside him, joining him in exploring the Bible and spending time with a Father who loves us. He has cheered me on as I have taken faltering steps into new ventures and new experiences with God. Gareth has let me run at my own pace. He has learned to run his own race while "circling back" to check on me. And when I've fallen, he has held out his hand of love, and helped me back up again, and inspired me to get back in the race.

This has worked both ways.

At different times in our marriage, we have been each other's pacesetters. As Gareth cheers me on and encourages me, his biggest goal is not that I would trust *him* more (though this has been a beautiful byproduct), but that I would trust *Jesus* more. When Gareth has fallen and not wanted to get back up, my aim is not that he seeks *my* approval when I help him, but for him to hear, "Look who's at the finish line. Jesus is waiting for you there. Don't stop now. Let's do this together."

We point each other to Jesus because only He can perfect our individual characters, our marriage, and most of all our faith.

Recently we did a marriage preparation class with a fabulous young couple. The material we walked through helped us as much as it helped them. In her book, *Marriage Revolution*[5] Nancy Houston opened our eyes to a new perspective. We commonly hear people say marriage is 50/50. Nancy suggests this should be a fluid percentage that always adds up to 100%. For instance, when I'm struggling, giving my usual 50 percent feels monumental. Gareth then steps in to make up the difference. So it becomes 70/30. Or when Gareth is laid low, I pick up the slack and it becomes 20/80. Of course, we are not designed to function at those levels for long periods of time, but what a great picture of sharing the load with someone for a portion of time, always reaching 100% with the help of our loving God.

My own journey of faith has been fun, and it's been hard. Don't let anyone ever tell you that being a Jesus follower is easy. It's not. There are days—and sometimes weeks and months—when I have to gather my courage and press in hard to the Jesus that I *know* is there, even when I can't seem to find Him. The image of a healthy marriage reminds me Jesus is my bridegroom. When I'm exhausted, He will carry me. When I'm enjoying His presence and celebrating life, Jesus joins me in that joy. When I'm lagging behind, the Holy Spirit encourages me to take one step at a time and to not stop the race.

And finally, I have learned that I have to *choose* marriage. I have to decide to love Gareth and to determine to act lovingly towards him. This often comes easily but sometimes feels impossible. And I have no doubt Gareth would say the same thing about being married to me! Some days I endlessly frustrate him, days when I disengage my "Jesus filter" and allow my mouth to have its way instead of reining it in. On those days, Gareth must *decide* to love me. Likewise, I have to teach my soul to need Gareth. I am fiercely independent, but marriage opposes that way of thinking. I can certainly be my own person, and Gareth fully supports and encourages that, but never at the expense of the "us" we have agreed upon.

This also applies to my relationship with Jesus. Jesus wants me to grow fully into the individual He's designed me to be, but not at the expense of a more intimate relationship with Him. If what I'm doing sacrifices my marriage or my relationship with Jesus, it is not something I should pursue.

I'm not perfect, but I seek the perfection that comes from being like Christ. Gareth's not perfect, but he too seeks the perfection that comes from being like Christ. Neither of us will attain this perfection until we see Jesus face to face. But in the meantime, it is our responsibility, as willing participants in the covenant of marriage, to point each other towards Jesus.

One last note: if you are a single person and reading this causes you pain, I am truly, deeply sorry. I pray that God will give you the desire of your heart. I also pray that you will be a beautiful expression of a pacesetter to someone to whom you are not married (a friend, a co-worker, a sibling). May you witness some exemplary examples of the marriage bond around you, and may *you* be a cheerleader to your friends and family because Father God calls us to live in encouraging and loving community. May you also find a trusted champion to continually point you back to the throne room of God.

———◇———

Holy Spirit, teach us to be great encouragers. Help us to always see you as the best goal. Lead us to love like You love and give like You give. Show us how to have You at the center of all we do so all will know our lives are Yours.
Amen.

Ten

Oil of Blessing

The Song:

Verse 1:
I sit at your feet, welcome guest at your table
Feeling your peace
And knowing you're able to save
You're able to save.
I'm welcomed right here at the feast of my Father
A child of the King
A friend of Messiah who saves
Messiah who saves.

Chorus 1:
So empty out your oil of blessing over me
Wash me with that fragrance of unending mercy
Pour out so much oil, till it drips down my face
And bless me with the honour, of my Saviour's embrace.

Verse 2:

I choose to be yours, every breath, every moment
So all that I am,
Will emanate fragrance of you
Fragrance of you
I want every drop, every speck of your essence
To flow through my life
And emanate fragrance of you
The fragrance of you.

(Chorus 1)

Verse 3:

I come to your throne as a child who's forgiven
And fall on my face,
With humble abandon and praise,
Abandon and praise
My life is my gift, nothing else I can give you
I bring you my all with humble abandon and praise
Abandon and praise.

Chorus 2:

I'll empty out my oil of worship over you
Wash you with the fragrance of unending gratitude
I'll pour out so much oil till there's nothing more
Giving my everything to the King I adore.

(Chorus 1)

The Story: Oil of Blessing

In that instant, she lost everything. Her retirement fund was gone. She squandered her inheritance and left nothing. She wept as she poured out every last drop of her future and her earthly security. She cried as she watched it run away and her heaving sobs were heard by all around. They frowned and whispered, as she withheld nothing, giving all in utter devotion.

He had taken the anointing oil and poured it everywhere. The sweet fragrance that gilded the air was both comforting and intoxicating. He took hold of his older brother strongly, lovingly embraced him, and then began to pour the anointing oil over his head. The oil began to wend its way skillfully around the twists and turns of his brother's hair. It didn't stop there. There was so much oil that it continued its passage past the end of the man's ringlets, dripping onto his abundant beard. The reverent awe with which he responded showed all around that his heart had been vastly enriched with this blessing.

Anointing. Blessing.

Two different stories wrapped in the same truth.

The first is the story of the lady we read about in Luke 7:36-50. There are other accounts of this meeting in all the gospels, and they differ slightly. But for our purpose, we are going to use this account in Luke's gospel. I encourage you to stop for a moment and read it.

She must have known who Jesus was because she clearly desired to see Him. Maybe she *was* a sinner but had found forgiveness in Jesus earlier while listening to Him teach truth. Or perhaps she was still living in darkness, and in that very moment when she came to meet Jesus in that room, His Light had drawn her out. Either way, her deliberate and calculated visit showed her deep devotion for Christ and recognition of her need for forgiveness.

This woman gave Jesus everything she had. She took a jar of perfumed oil to give to Jesus. The oil was extremely valuable; many people kept such oil for their own burial, or for the burial of a loved one. This was the *best* she had to give. But that was not all she gave Jesus, for she also anointed Him with her tears.

Just imagine the scene.

She was so compelled to see Jesus, she gathered up her courage and entered the room full of raucous men, uninvited and unwanted. Not only was she a known sinner, she was obviously a woman in a world dominated by men. Her yearning to be with the Savior led her to step over the hurdles of manners, requirement, status, and position. She had to anoint her King, and nothing was going to stop her.

The second story is Moses anointing Aaron in the temple. We read this account in Leviticus 8:1-13. Read it before we go on.

Aaron was called by God. He and his sons were set apart to be holy and play an important role in the lives of the Israelites. Aaron was to be the very first High Priest. This anointing, although bestowed by his brother, came directly from God. In Scripture, anointing with oil was God's expression of His unique calling. We also see kings and prophets set apart in the Old Testament by anointing.

In one case we have the pouring out of oil over Jesus. We see the woman bring her own gift of oil, and we watch as she empties it with loving abandon. This is her act of all-embracing worship. In the other case we have Aaron who is being set apart and called out by God. He is receiving his "you are appointed" anointing.

Anointing. Blessing.

When I wrote "Oil of Blessing," I was worshiping the Father at the piano. I was praying, singing, and thanking Him for allowing us to worship Him in freedom. The phrase "pour out so much oil 'til it drips down my face" became my refrain as I asked Holy Spirit to fill me again as I worshiped Him. Of course, this image had come to me from the story of Aaron. However, as I pondered this, I realized that although Aaron ended up in worship of God, this anointing act was not specifically an act of worship but an act of God giving Aaron his assignment. In that moment my attention shifted from what I could give God, to what He has so graciously given me.

I became overwhelmed by the truth that He has called me by name (Isaiah 43:1). And that as He called me, He did not hold back on all the blessing that He wanted to bestow on me. Even as I write this, I am overawed again that God gave *all*. He poured out His blessing on me in such great quantities that it will, just as the oil did on Aaron, drip down my face.

When I was a teenager, I wrote this poem:

> When God touches me
> He doesn't use just His fingertips.
> He reaches out His whole strong hand
> To encompass me with love.

> When God calls for me
> He doesn't just beckon with one finger.
> He stands with arms open
> Ready to receive me with true warmth.
> When God waits for me
> He doesn't use a stopwatch.
> He sits in perfect peace
> Until I stand on holy ground.
> When God gives a blessing
> He doesn't use a thimble.
> He gathers every river
> And gently pours it over me.

You see, our God is one of *abundance*. He is one of *more*. He is a Father of *immeasurable* goodness (Ephesians 3:20). He is the good Father who gave His only son, Jesus (John 3:16-17).

As I read that poem again all these years later (I hate to actually count how *many* years!) I am still struck by that truth. God has more! God *is* more! God is the most perfect giver you'll ever hope to know. He gives out of His abundance. Think about that for a second. He gives out of His abundance! How much abundance does our God have? He owns the cattle on a thousand hills, and every bird on every mountain is His (Psalm 50:7-15).

Like the woman in Luke, my only response is thankful worship. That is all I have to give. This woman took a representation of her "all" by bringing that which was most valuable to her, and completely emptied it over the feet of Jesus. She did not pour it over His head because she was acting as His servant, worshipping as she bowed at His feet. She poured out not only her perfumed oil, but also her salty tears. And why those tears? I imagine that she was, as I have been on so many occasions, overcome by the sheer weight of truth that she was forgiven. Forgiven! Everything in her past was wiped away. Everything! I want my humble reaction to be the same, to enthusiastically embrace the forgiveness offered to me.

And my only response is worship! I will pour out every ounce of me. I will empty my "jar of perfume" over the feet of my Master, Jesus. I will anoint my King with the worship of my life as that is all I can give Him. The good news is the worship of my life is all Jesus wants me to give Him!

These two pictures have become forever entwined in my mind. First, the picture of Father God anointing me, sending me out as His, pouring His *all* over me and calling me chosen and priest (1 Peter 2:9). And then, the picture of me sitting at the feet of Jesus, welcomed to His side, invited to eat at His table, pouring out all of my worship over His feet.

What if, as I pour out my oil of worship over Him, Jesus is at the same time pouring out His oil of anointing over me? What if my oil and His oil mingle in a beautiful puddle of election and adoration at the foot of the Throne?

We can rest in the enveloping, surrounding embrace of our Lord as we pour out all we are and submit to worshiping Him in complete abandon.

———————⟡———————

King Jesus, You desire my worship. Teach me anew what it means to pour out every drop of my devotion over You. Show me again how You love to bless me with Your majestic abundance. And as I worship You, Father, may I be so covered in Your prevailing fragrance that everywhere I go I will be reminded that I am Yours, and You are mine.
Amen.

Epilogue

I love a story with a happy ending—that wonderful satisfaction as the plot gathers beautifully together, everything neat and tidy. The reader breathes a contented sigh of deep gratification, and all is well with the world.

But maybe you're the reader who prefers the massive plot twist? Just when you absolutely knew you had it all figured out, the story spirals away from its seemingly intended path, leaving you gasping in awe as your mind unravels. The presumptions in the vaults of your imagination are dragged away, crashing into a completely different reality, and yet you relish this thrill of the unexpected!

Others delight in the cliffhanger. Nothing is certain, no one is safe, and there is no solace for your creative mind in this perpetual state of speculation. And in your opinion, the thrill of the unknown leaves you thirsting for the sequel!

As you turn the last page of this book, my deepest hope is that you experience all three of those emotions.

I want you to know you have a "happy ending" right now. When you acknowledge and look for the power of Jesus in your life, you have absolutely everything you need to ***stand***. Right now, full stop, period, enough, that's it! I pray the stories and scriptures you have read will convince you that you are equipped, you are loved, you are able and therefore you are willing to take up your position—today. Everything Jesus has done for you is already finished. Our Father has no more plans to think up for you—He designed and finalized His specific plans for you before He even created the universe. Your faith is His gift to you, beautifully wrapped with all the perfection Jesus won on the cross. So you can ***stand*** and believe that not only is God in control, but He is in control for your good and the good of the Kingdom. There's more to come, but you can live in the security of the happy ending when you joyously surrender to the King of Kings.

However, I also long for you to experience the exhilaration of the "plot twist." I often imagine I have the best ideas for the most effective outcomes to situations. I think I'm pretty good at knowing where this or that plot will lead, only to discover—again—how severely my ideas and plans are lacking. My wisdom is finite in the most obvious ways because I can only "see in part" (1 Corinthians 13:12b). So,

Epilogue

when my Father reveals to me a plot twist, He reminds me again (and again) that He is perfect and all His plans for me are good. And in those instances, He once again affords me the heavenly opportunity to ***stand*** and submit everything to Jesus. When the ground feels uneven and the path unexpectedly turns, I can plant my feet firmly in the Truth and take my stance. I remind myself that this plot twist is no surprise to God, and it is a chance for me to exercise my faith again, for it was our Heavenly Author's good plan all along. I can safely stand upon the promises and authenticity of God.

The "cliffhanger" is perhaps the most terrifying and thrilling of all. I hope you feel so safe with the Father that you will not only allow Him to lead you into the uncertainty of the cliffhanger, but that you will willingly embrace its excitement. I hope you have experienced new intimacy with Jesus, moving you to become bolder in your faith, more courageous in how you interact with others who don't yet know Jesus, extra daring in the prayers you pray, bravely extravagant in the way you give to others. My desire is that your foundation in Jesus, and your belief in His power, have been reinforced in such a way that you are no longer focused on how each chapter of your book will turn out, but instead motivated by a permanent stance of steady faith in the fact that your book ends in victory! I pray you will experience glorious cliffhangers, knowing "faith is confidence in what we hope for and assurance about what we do not see" (Hebrews 11:1).

Assurance and confidence often exist alongside uncertainty. This uncomfortable combination will propel us into a different level of faith. Let us be those who are stirred to pray, speak, act, and to live a "Jesus life" with such confidence that we are not primarily concerned about what happens when we turn the page. I want us all to be willing to **stand** up for what is right without first weighing the consequences. I want us all to pray into the most troubling and exhausting situations without the burden of the "what if's" hampering our freedom. May each of us wholeheartedly surrender to the love and power of our Great God so when we don't see the answers, we will allow the tension of cliffhangers and **stand** anyway.

Your story will continue to be filled to the brim with happy endings, plot twists, and cliffhangers. Your feet are safely and firmly planted upon the Rock of our Salvation, simultaneously standing on Truth and moving in faith.

So dear Reader,

May your heart have the courage to wait for Jesus. May you allow your soul the space to find perfect rest in a Savior who loves you. May you find yourself forever exalting and adoring your Shepherd King.

I pray your heart will deeply trust God, and you will have a resilient confidence that He will move. I pray you will be filled with such awe and amazement in our God that you will be compelled to praise Him with the worship of your heart. I'm asking Holy Spirit to prompt you to live every moment to the glory of the Father of all days. I want you to be brave enough to pray the prayer you think you can't believe, and to settle yourself on the fact that Jesus is the perfecter of your faith. And finally, I am asking the Father to so richly drench you with the oil of His blessing that it drips down your face and spills out into every area of your existence.

Stand.

Don't be moved.

Stand and see what God will do.

Love,
Sharon

References

Chapter 1

[1] Browne, Thomas J.. *American Physical Education Review 1916*, Volume 21, p176. Thesis presented by Browne in June 1915

Chapter 3

[2] Chesterton, G.K.. *Father Brown* story *The Hammer of God*. Find this and other stories in *The Collected Works of G.K. Chesterton, Vol 12*

Chapter 4

[3] Henry, Matthew. *Commentary of the Whole Bible* (Peabody, MA. Hendrickson Publishers, 2008), 2 Chronicles Chapter 7, Verses 12-22 II.

[4] Nee, Watchman. *The Spiritual Man*, Volume 2, Part 6, The Normalcy of the Spirit: A Spirit of Power.

Chapter 9

[5] Houston, Nancy. *Marriage Revolution 8-Week Study Guide*. (Southlake, TX. Gateway Create Publishing, 2014).

Stand, the CD

To find Sharon's accompanying album, *Stand* go to www.61-Things.com, iTunes or Google Play.

Printed in Great Britain
by Amazon